FIELD DRESSINGS

——————— BY ———————

STRETCHER BEARER

——————— FRANCE ———————

1916 - 17 - 18 - 19

The Poems of Alick Lewis Ellis

FIELD DRESSINGS

—— BY ——

STRETCHER BEARER

—— FRANCE ——

1916 - 17 - 18 - 19

The Poems of Alick Lewis Ellis

BROWN
DOG
BOOKS

Published under licence by Brown Dog Books and
The Self-Publishing Partnership, 7 Green Park Station, Bath BA1 1JB

www.selfpublishingpartnership.co.uk

ISBN: 978-1-78545-285-7

Cover design by Andrew Prescott
Internal design by Andrew Easton

Printed and bound by CPI Group (UK) Ltd, Croydon, CR0 4YY

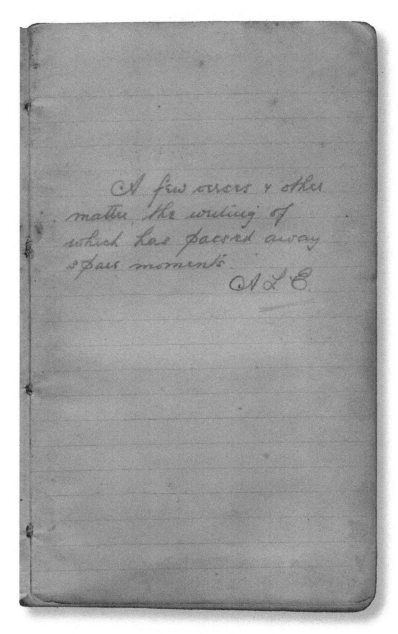

A few errors & other
matter, the writing of
which has passed away
spare moments.
A L E.

The introduction page from the original "Field Dressings"

Contents

Preface

The discovery of the original 'Field Dressings by Stretcher Bearer' came as a total surprise to the current Ellis family and the literary endeavour of our great uncle, Alick Lewis Ellis was completly unknown to us. We are therefore indebted to the anonymous person who handed the original book of poetry into the Herts at War Project[1], with a note saying it had been found in the loft of a house during renovation and 'may be of interest to you'. Dan Hill of the Herts at War Project, tracked down Alick's nephew and closest living relative, Robert 'Bob' Ellis to whom he planned to return the book. At that time Bob Ellis was too ill to receive the book, so it was returned to us, his children who accepted it on his behalf, with the handover being shown on the ITN 6 O'clock news in October 2017. Sadly, Bob Ellis passed away in late 2017 so was never able to see his Uncle's work published.

In bringing these new works to print, we have endeavoured to transcribe them as accurately as possible attempting to keep the format, style and punctuation close to that of the original. For example, the ampersand is used throughout much of the original text, and has been retained in the transcription. Any errors in transcription or omissions that remain are therefore entirely due to us. Occasional obvious spelling mistakes have been altered, but these are at an absolute minimum. In one poem 'Major Wallace MC (and bar)', an editorial decision was made to change one word in the original line 'A white man to the end' to 'A right man to the end'. The original meaning of the phrase 'white man' at the time of Alick's writing is consistent with the positive message of the poem, but a present day interpretation could be considered controversial, and so the alteration was made.

The RAMC, of which Alick was a part, has been instrumental in helping to define, manage and treat the full range of battlefield injuries and traumas. From 'shell shock' of the WW1 trenches to the modern understanding of PTSD the RAMC has been in the vanguard. To recognise the role that the RAMC has had and continues to have, it is only fitting that a proportion of the profits from this book should be used in support of suitable PTSD charities. The charities that will be supported are Combat Stress[2] and Veterans With Dogs[3].

Peter Ellis
Pat Russell
(Great Nephew and Great Niece to Alick Ellis)

In support of

(2) *https://www.combatstress.org.uk/*

(3) *https://veteranswithdogs.org.uk/*

Biography -Alick Lewis Ellis

1887-1953

Alick Lewis Ellis was born on 19th January 1887 to John and Susan Jane Ellis of Terrington St Clement in Norfolk, England. One of 10 children, he had 2 elder and one younger sister, and 3 elder and 3 younger brothers.

Little is known of his early life, but it is thought that he attended the local Terrington School with his brothers and sisters where he received a good but unremarkable education. The Ellis family had for several generations been shopkeepers, butchers or grocers, and his parents were no different. The Census returns for 1891-1911 showed John Ellis to initially be a grocer, then by 1911 the village postmaster. The registered address of Vine House, Terrington St Clement, in 1901 was to provide important information tying Alick's recently discovered works to this family.

By the 1911 Census Alick appeared to be following in the family tradition and was registered on that Census night in Terrington St Clement as a self-employed (own account) grocer aged 24, whose residence was Greenhithe (in Kent). On the face of it, Kent appears to be quite a significant move for the son of a village postmaster from a small Norfolk village.

Why had he moved to Greenhithe in Kent? Well, the answer lies apparently with his widowed sister-in-law May Ellis, formerly married to Walter Percy Ellis, one of Alick's older brothers. May Ellis (formerly May Russell) was born and brought up in Hoddesdon, Herts, but by 1901 was recorded as a draper's assistant living at 23 Station Road, Greenhithe in Kent with her widowed sister and her employer's family. In the 2011 Census she is recorded as being a widowed grocer at 20 Station Road in Greenhithe, Kent, having married Walter Percy Ellis in the interim. Interestingly, Alick's younger brother Charles Wesley Ellis was also registered at 20 Station Road in 2011 as a grocer's assistant. By the outbreak of war in 1914 Greenhithe had become a pivotal place for several members of the Ellis family.

Alick volunteered for Territorial Army service at the Duke of York's Headquarters, Chelsea on the 4th February 1915, giving his address as 20 Station Road, Greenhithe, Kent. The registration paper is damaged, but much of the information is easily decipherable. Along with his regimental numbers it is clear he volunteered into the 3rd Ldn/ (rest unreadable). It is assumed to be the 3rd London Field Ambulance of the Royal Army Medical Corps (RAMC), part of the 56th (1st London) Division, who were based at the Duke of York's Barracks in Chelsea. The registration paper has 'Imperial' handwritten on it, indicating that he had agreed to overseas service.

Alick's registration papers for the 3rd London Field Ambulance

The 56th Division is confirmed by Alick's writing in 'Field Dressings'. There is a glowing tribute to the fighting worth of his fellow comrades in two very different poems entitled '56th London Division'. His earliest works are finished off with a small 'doodle', which over time appear to evolve into the insignia of the 56th Division, the sword symbolising the martyrdom of Paul the Apostle taken from the coat of arms of the City of London. Another of the poems from 'Field Dressings' is a tribute to an officer 'Major Wallace MC (with bar), 2/3rd Lon Fld Amb, Killed in Action 27/3/18'. The name, rank, date and confirmation that he was killed in action all tie in with the unit's official daily war diary, so from this we can reasonably assume that Alick, too, served in the 2/3rd London Field Ambulance.

Little is known about the specific wartime experiences of Alick, except those picked out from his poetry. He left no diary or other record and was not known to have confided in any friends or relatives. It is assumed that he served with the 2/3rd London Field Ambulance throughout the campaign on the Western Front, supporting the 169th Brigade of the 56th Division at its numerous actions.

Its first actions were at Gommecourt, Ginchy, Flers-Courcelette, Morval and Transloy Ridges, all phases of the Somme in 1916. In 1917, the division saw action at the Battle of Arras, then the Third Battle of Ypres (Passchendaele), and by the end of the year several phases of the Cambrai operations. 1918 saw no respite with action at the First and Second Battles of the Somme. The Battle of the Scarpe a phase of the Second Battles of Arras soon followed as summer reached its height. Further engagements at the Battle of the Canal du Nord and Cambrai saw the breaching of the Hindenburg Line before the Division took part in the Final Advance in Picardy. By November 1918, the 56th was finally withdrawn for a rest. Before its demobilisation in May 1919, the Division was in existence for 1010 days, with 330 days at rest, 195 in quiet sectors, 385 in active sectors and 100 days in battle [4].

Specific battles and some actions are referred to throughout the verses. Cambrai features prominently in the poem 'Victory', while other battles and actions fought by the 56th Division are mentioned in 'Can you forget'. The Palestine campaign also gets a mention in 'Can you forget' the theatre of war where Alick's elder brother, Clarence Allen Ellis, was also serving with the RAMC in the 2/6th London Field Ambulance. These varied references to different parts of the Western Front and the carefully chosen military and political quotations in 'All men are liars' suggest that, in spite of his village school education, Alick was a well-informed writer.

Although none of the poems in 'Field Dressings' are individually dated, it is assumed that they were all conceived and written during the 1916-1919 period, as indicated on the title page. Three additional poems written by Alick have been discovered in the belongings of his closest relatives. Two of these were found amongst the papers of his brother and fellow RAMC member Clarence Allen, and one, 'Real Greatness', was written for and given to his nephew Robert Ellis, Clarence's younger son. These later poems are perhaps a little less reflective of the life in the trenches than those in 'Field Dressings', are certainly more forward-looking, and are believed to have been written at various times after the war. One of these, 'Victory' (the second poem entitled Victory), is signed Alick L Ellis, the signature matching that on the Army registration paper.

(4) http://www.longlongtrail.co.uk/army/order-of-battle-of-divisions/56th-1st-london-division/

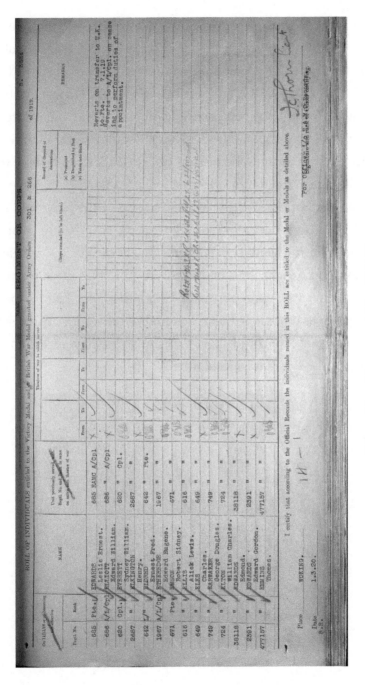

War medal entitlement record for Alick Ellis

War records show that Alick, like all soldiers serving overseas, was entitled to the Victory Medal and the British War Medal. His official entry in the war medal entitlement record has "Rtd 1743 KR CRVBdl 27.6.23/8071 adt" written next to it. This suggests that the medals were returned, possibly unclaimed at the address to which they were sent, and under Kings Regulations 1743 they were eventually sent away to be broken up. Did Alick not receive them, or did he return them himself – disillusioned having witnessed and recorded the horrors of the trenches? However, the term 'adt' at the end of the inscription refers to adjustment, so possibly there was an issue with the medals or a correction to be made – perhaps in the name inscription. It is interesting to note that the next man in the document (the similarly named Pte. Elks) also had his medals returned – was it possible that the medals were mixed up and sent to the wrong men. We could speculate, but as the medals cannot now be traced, it will remain speculation.

Alick Ellis – back row centre, best man at his brother's wedding

(Photograph from Ellis family archive)

Not much is known about Alick's life after he left the RAMC, and there are few concrete records or references. He was the best man at his brother Clarence Allen's wedding to Alice May Dawson in October 1921, with photographs showing Alick along with the married couple and bridesmaids. For such a formal photograph, there are suggestions of people trying to suppress a smile or two.

At some point he moved to Bedford; we don't really know when. Electoral records show he lived at 46 Foster Hill Road, Bedford, from 1932 to his death in 1953 with his landlady Ada Bannister.

In the late 1930s and early 1940s Alick was visited on occasion by his two nephews Peter and Robert (Bob) Ellis, sons of Clarence and Alice May Ellis to whom Alick was best man in 1921. Peter and Bob would cycle from Terrington St Clement in Norfolk to Bedford to visit Alick for a holiday. It was during one of these visits that Bob received the poem 'Real Greatness' from Alick.

Family recollections of that period are a little vague, but it is believed that Alick worked in various local supermarkets in Bedford. It was perhaps a throwback to the family business and Alick's time as a grocer in Greenhithe before the outbreak of the Great War.

The last photograph and record of Alick that we can find is his attendance at his brother Clarence Allen's second wedding (his first wife passing away in 1944) in May 1953, 6 months to the day before Alick sadly passed away. Alick Lewis Ellis passed away on the 20th of November 1953, in Bedford. So what happened to his book of poems and how were they discovered? No one seems to really know, except that the book was anonymously handed in to Dan Hill at the Herts at War Project in 2017, with a note saying it had been found during a house renovation and 'may be of interest to you'. Perhaps it was from 46 Foster Hill Road, or perhaps an earlier address; we may never know. To whoever found it and generously handed it in we say a heartfelt thank-you. Dan Hill tracked down Alick's closest living relatives through the name and address at the front of 'Field Dressings', 'Mrs Ellis, Vine House, Terrington St Clement', through the Terrington St Clement History Group with whom the family still has a connection. 'Field Dressings' then made its final journey back to the Ellis family on Wednesday 26th July 2017, where it was presented to the family by Dan Hill of the Herts at War Project, to whom we will always be very grateful.

Poems

Extract from Unit Orders

Clothing

Any man not wishing to draw winter underclothing must report same in writing to Orderly Room.

I submit the following reply as being a change from the crude official manner with which one is accustomed to, corresponds with Orderly Room

"In accordance with orders routine,
Relating to health & hygiene,
I have no need to draw
Vest & pants from the store
I've a surplus of same sweet & clean"

"An unknown British soldier"

I
"An unknown British soldier"
I read on a rough cross of wood
By the side of a shell-marked roadway
Stained with a nation's blood
No monument of marble
Gave a name to that human clay
But the golden rays of a setting sun
Kissed that rough cross of wood on its way

II
An unknown British soldier
In that grave all alone & forlorn
Put down on the lists as "missing"
(for such is the Government form)
But a Mother, Wife, Sweetheart is waiting
A letter or knock at the door
Praying, though tears may be falling
Oh God! bring him safe back once more

III

An unknown British soldier
Lies, unknown to his fellows on earth
But where darkness is banished for ever
There an angel records a new birth
So Mother or Wife bear your sorrow
And sweetheart smile through your tears
For your loved one is known over yonder
Where time is not measured in years
He is there in that City Eternal
No longer in pain or unknown
Where hardship & death are forgotten
And hatred & bloodshed have flown

IV

Hope on & have faith, for the darkness
Shall give place to the heavenly day
When the mists of the earth shall vanish
In the light of Eternal ray
Then the Angels & Archangels
Will point him out with pride
True Unknown British soldier
Who for Right & Freedom died

Untitled - (Title pencilled out)

Life is a play, we are players,
Each one is allotted a part,
Though varied the talent among us,
Let us carry it through with good heart.
Let each act as it comes be the better,
And the last one of all hold the crown,
We shall know then the Great Judge's verdict,
When death brings our life's curtain down.

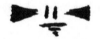

A Vision

I had a dream of the Great Beyond
That land behind the veil
I stood at the gates of the City
Where lustre & light do not pale
I saw an host of Angels
A countless white-robed throng
And heard the voice of thousands
Swelling out the "glad new song"
For the gates of the City were opened
Not ajar, but flung open wide
And the ransomed stood to welcome
The souls who had crossed the tide

Then I heard a muffled marching
Of a throng steadfast & bold
Drawing nearer to the City gates
Nearer their crown of gold
And I saw earth's shattered legions
Armies of the nations slain
Pressing onwards as a river
Free from hardship strife & pain

Through the high triumphal arches
To the courtyard of the King
Foes on earth but now as brothers
Death has levelled envy's sling
Robes of white now veiled their bodies
Battered, torn by wars grim game
Faces that on earth were tortured
Now illumined bear His name

And I saw this vast host gathered
As the sheep when in the fold
Waiting for their Captain's welcome
There before the throne of gold
Then the heavenly music thundered
As the waves on rock bound shore
To the hymn the Angels chanted
Peace and rest for evermore

And a light of dazzling glory
Brighter than Earth's noonday glare
Heralded the Judge's coming
To the "great tribunal" there
Then a hush, a low soft murmur
As the cooing of a dove
Came upon that vast assembly
As they saw the God of Love

Then the voice that countless ages
Spoke & made Earth's land & seas
Filled that Paradise unmeasured
As a gentle summer breeze
"Faithful servants be ye welcome
Ye who lived & fought & died
For the right of weaker brothers
And who now have crossed the tide

Ye shall wear the crown of glory
Whose lustre shall not fade away
Ye have run the race undaunted
And not fallen by the way
There are many mansions ready
Which I have prepared for you
Well done all ye good & faithful
Ye have used my talents true"

I awoke from my dream and around me
Seemed a light that was not of the earth
And my soul rose in praise to my Maker
For the promise of Heavenly birth.

"Victory"

Bells were rung in many churches in honour of the Cambrai victory.

Daily Papers

There's a winding line of stretchers each with its shattered load
Coming slowly from the trenches along a shell-marked road
Hear the groans & watch the blood flow, see the havoc of the shells
And this is called a victory for this they rung the bells

See the groups of walking wounded who progress as best they can
Limping, struggling slowly onward helped by the stronger man
With clothing torn & faces pained & blood their path to show
But let the bells ring loud & clear its victory you know

There are heaps of dead in the trenches & out in "no man's land"
'Tis not for them a flowered grave tended by loving hand
There'll be vacant chairs in many homes in England's hills & dells
But still this is a victory for they have rung the bells

See this comrade of mine who has fallen he stood by my side at dawn
I have sewn his cold clay in a blanket fit coffin for grim waifair's storm
And I think of a wife who is waiting & a babe who its father will miss
Yet the bells were rung in our churches for such a victory as this

O Christ of a thousand Churches God of a nation's best
Look down & forgive the people & grant the fallen rest
Where flesh & blood now wrestle O grant the birds may sing
And peace be the greatest victory & then our bells shall ring

Wounded carried by mule. (Photograph from Ellis family archive)

Training & Reality

It really was a waste of time when
training for the fray
The orders we had bawled at us so many
times each day
And the sergeant's voice would bellow if we
seemed inclined to slack
"Just hold your bloomin' heads up & throw
your shoulders back"

But now we're in the trenches where the
shells & bullets sing
The command the sergeant gives us is
quite another thing
For if we try to follow out our train-
ing there's a furore
And we hear a voice of warning
"Keep your d —— d heads down"

Training & Reality

It really was a waste of time when training for the fray
The orders we had bawled at us so many times each day
And the sergeant's voice would bellow if we seemed inclined to slack
"Just hold your bloomin' heads up & throw your shoulders back"

But now we're in the trenches where the shells & bullets sing
The command the sergeant gives us is quite another thing
For if we try to follow out our training there's a frown
And we hear a voice of warning "Keep you d____d heads down"

Issues

The day I met the girl I loved
(I called her "Ruby Queen")
And that she had a "Classic" pose
In "'arf a mo'" was seen

She wore a "Swastika" for luck
And a neat "Woodbine" trimmed hat
She was sweeter far than "Honey Dew"
And she nursed an old "Black Cat"

She told me that my love would "Flag"
But from her I got a jar
For she went in a "Pinnace" one day for a trip
Side by side with a big "Red Hussar"

I felt that a shadow was dimming "Life's Rays"
When she posted this note on to me
"Will you act as "Chairman" at my wedding feast?
With love, your old flame B.D.V."

RAMC billet in the UK (Photograph from Ellis family archive)

Revenge

When this bloomin' war is over & I reach my native land,
I shall play the role of villain with a great revenge in hand,
I may get hung for murder but just take my word I'll risk it,
For I'm going to find the blinkin' man who made the Army biscuit.

Revenge

When this bloomin' war is over & I
reach my native land,
I shall play the role of william with a
great revenge in hand,
I may get hung for murder but just
take my word I'll risk it,
For I'm going to find the blinkin'
man who made the army biscuit.

Tommy's Christmas

There ain't no carol singers,
And there ain't no joyful bells,
But the bullets do the singin',
And the music comes from shells.

There ain't no holly hangin',
'Cos there ain't no marble 'alls,
But just a blinkin' dugout,
In which yer often crawls.

What! Mistletoe? Gawd blim'me,
There ain't no one to kiss,
And we don't get time for spoonin',
In such a place as this.

Yer can't get a bloomin' turkey,
Or a puddin' 'ot & sweet,
But a 'ard & tasteless biscuit,
And a tin o' bully meat.

Yer can't even get a swaller,
Of good old English beer,
But they gives yer as a favour,
A smell o' rum out 'ere.

But I ain't a goin' to grumble
That ain't my bloomin' style,
As long as the kids & missis,
Can 'ave a good time & smile.

So I thinks of my people in Blighty,
And wish 'em as I stand 'ere,
A jolly good time at Christmas,
And a blinkin' 'appy New Year.

"Tommy's" Manners (when on leave)

1

You call him a low-down fellow,
That figure in Khaki you see,
As he passes your way light-headed & gay,
From those trenches just over the sea.
You see him come out of the gin shop,
And stagger along the street,
With a rollicking song as he rolls along,
His balance a wonderful feat.

2

You see him come out of a brothel,
You mark him down as a beast,
And you there & then to your fellow men,
Consider him one of the least.
You think him devoid of all manners,
Yes, coarse when compared to your scale,
And you think & say in your Christian way,
He is really beyond the pale.

3

Ah! you who set up as judges,
Upon him who your virtues may lack,
Just pause for awhile from your cynical style,
And not class all colour as black,
But list to the tale I will tell you,
Of the life lived by him whom you scorn,
And when you have heard your thoughts may be stirred,
Your light of forgiveness may dawn.

4

He has stood in the mud of the trenches,
Exposed to the winter's full blast,
He has heard the sharp "twang" as the swift bullets sang,
Expecting each breath was his last,
His food would not grace England's tables,
Or his method of eating be great,
But crouched in a trench his knees as a bench,
Will give an idea of his state.

5

He has been where the ground heaves & trembles,
To the burst of the murderous shell,
He has seen the blood flow making red, winter's snow,
He has passed through the fires of Hell,
He has seen the life's-blood of his comrades,
As crimson, a pool on the ground,
In the heat of the brain he has slaughtered as Cain,
As Death with his scythe reaped around.

6

He has missed the sweet smiles of good women,
The softening influence of these,
He has seen awful sights in the long unknown nights,
When you sat in comfort & ease,
He has mixed with all sorts & conditions,
With those who blaspheme & who curse,
He has slept in the rain & marched when in pain,
'Till the goodness in him turns to worse.

7

Examine yourself you who judge him,
Remember the life that he leads
Change places with him where temtation to sin,
Is stronger than passions or creeds.
It is easy enough to be perfect,
When life all around you is good,
But the morals you hold would perhaps lose their gold,
If your future was slaughter & blood.

8

Would you be a saint full of virtues,
If you lived as a beast day by day?
Would your morals be high & your thoughts reach the sky,
If long years of war were your play?
If you knew, as he knows, that too swiftly,
The leave that he has will be past,
And you knew that again you would hear bullets rain,
This visit perhaps be your last.

9

O forgive him, that figure in khaki,
He lives in the fires of hate,
Allow him a right to be merry & bright,
Though his morals may be a low state.
Remember a man who is starving,
Will greedily eat of the bread,
And the man who is free from over the sea,
Forgive him for lightness of head.
He is passing through hardship & danger,
In order your life may be free,
And perhaps out of sight there's a big streak of white,
As he thinketh in head so is he.

10

Just think were you tempted as he is,
Your goodness to his might be dim,
So forgive him & say in your prayers day by day,
"My God, I thank you for him".

The false prophet

Horatio! Horatio!* I pray you do not weep,
I know your heart is breaking your hurt is very deep,
But dry those tears I ask you the sight of them gives pain,
You backed Russia as a winner & you lost, but try again.

Rumania! Rumania! was that the word you used?
I see it now that leader which in "John Bull" I perused,
You said she was so useful with her oil & with her grain,
But although the Germans got it John, don't cry, but try again.

Watch Italy! Watch Italy! a splendid phrase was that,
I felt like shouting out "Hurrah!" & throwing up my hat,
For you told us to the Allies she would prove a splendid gain,
I don't say you're a liar, but buck up, & try again.

Ah Christmastime! Ah Christmastime! this fighting would be o'er,
Then, Sir Douglas Haig had told you would be the end of war,
But still "old Fritz" is busy but I won't call you insane,
You're a d____d bad hand at guessing, never mind, but try again.

Editor's note: Assumed to be either Horatio Herbert Kitchener, Secretary of State for War, or quite possibly Horatio Bottomley, British MP, prominent speaker, fraudster and editor of the popular John Bull magazine at the time of the Great War.

"Cuba has declared war on the Central Empires" - *Daily Mail*

In the palace of Potsdam a great company met,
There were Emperors, Rulers, & Kings,
They had met by command of the Kaiser 'tis said,
To discuss on the outlook of things.

They toasted an health to success of their cause,
And another to Russia's farewell,
They lifted their glasses to Hindenburg too,
And determined to give England hell.

"We have met here today" the All-Highest said,
"For victory to us is quite near,
There's Britain & France & America left,
But from them we have nothing to fear."

"We've beaten Rumania & knocked Russia out,
And Italy reels on her feet,
While Uncle Sam's men will chip in too late,
For by then we'll have England dead beat".

So they settled themselves to be merry & gay,
And the rafters of Potsdam soon rang,
To the medley of voices & words of good cheer,
As they feasted, & toasted, & sang.

But their spirits soon fell as into the room,
A messenger rushed out of breath,
And he handed a message to Kaiser Wilhelm,
Who read with a face pale as death.

In a voice low & hushed he read it aloud,
And his hearers all listened in awe,
Then the floor shook & trembled & nearly gave way,
As they fell in a heap on the floor.

The Crown Prince's head rested on his Pa's feet,
And the Sultan of Turkey was found,
Supporting himself with the aid of a chair,
His fez badly crushed on the ground,

Poor "Ferdy the foxy" with his eyes closed & pale,
Was really a pitiful wreck,
As he partly reclined with his fat arms around,
The Emperor of Austria's neck.

It was just at this moment that Hindenburg came,
With a martial step into the room,
Then he searched all around for the cause of that scene,
Which had put all the "heads" in a swoon.
And there tightly clenched in the great War Lord's hand,
Was the message which he quickly saw,
Then he read out its words & fainted away,
For Cuba had just declared war.

Motorised field ambulances (Photograph from Ellis family archive)

Untitled

I saw the rising sun
Peep o'er the hills splendid in all its majesty,
I read its message clear,
It seemed to say to me
          "The day is here"

I saw the setting sun
Sink silently beyond the hills, like a golden ray,
I watched its fading light,
To me it seemed to say,
          "Remember night"

I saw the rising sun
Peep o'er the hills in all its splendid majesty,
I read its message clear,
It seemed to say to me,
                    "The day is here".

I saw the setting sun
Sink silently beyond the hills, a golden ray,
I watched its fading light,
To me it seemed to say —
                    "Remember night."

"All men are liars"
Psalm

"I know those trenches"

George V

"The war will be over by Xmas (1917)"

Horatio Bottomley

"The war is all but won"

Gen Smuts

"The men said to me (at Messines) 'We don't want to be relieved'"

Beach Thomas

"I found the men in the best of spirits"

Ben Tillett M.P.

"They (the troops) seemed to regard the battle as a joke"

Hamilton Fyfe

"Yonder"

What have you seen out there my boy,
Where the lust for blood is keen,
And men meet men with passion roused,
I ask what have you seen?

Mother mine! Over yonder,
I have seen all nature's dress,
Withered & scorched by the cannons blast,
To a barren wilderness.
I have seen the blood of the sinner,
Mingle with blood of the just,
And men like unto His image,
Slay brother with awful lust?

What have you heard out there my boy,
Where the earth with noise is stirred,
And the great hills shake with man made force,
I ask what have you heard?

Mother mine! Over yonder,
I have heard the great guns roar,
As the thunder of all ages,
On a mighty storm-cloud's door,
I have heard the curse of sinner,

The prayers of a widow's son,
And groans of a fallen brother,
As the course of life is run.

What have you felt out there my boy,
Where all goodness seems to melt,
And black deeds stamp the devil's power,
I ask what have you felt?

Mother mine! Over yonder,
I have felt the hand of Death,
Brush my life in its passing,
I have felt his fiery breath.
The sins of my past have risen,
As tide on the golden sand,
I have felt the Reaper's presence,
The touch of that awful hand.

What have you done out there my boy,
In the darkness or mid-day sun,
When duty called you to play the man,
I ask what have you done?

Mother mine! Over yonder,
I have done my duty well,
In the heat of the bloody battle,
In the raging fires of Hell.

I have done my best for my fellows,
Who have fallen of wounds by the way,
And the best of my best has been given,
To save, when the shells fail to slay.

What have you thought out there my boy,
When you for hope have sought,
In the silent hours or bitter fight,
I ask what have you thought?

Mother mine! Over yonder,
I have thought of my native land,
Of loved ones waiting patiently,
For the clasp of a dear one's hand,
I have thought of a loving Mother,
And a Father dear at home,
An old arm chair by the fireside,
When peace calls me over the foam.
I have thought of the Heavenly City,
Of Him who was nailed to the cross,
And my soul has been lifted & strengthened,
I have thought of the good in the dross.

What might have been

When the weight of years is a heavy load,
As you near the end of life's rough road,
When the buoyancy of youth is past,
And the sands of time are sinking fast,
What memories come before you keen,
As you think of years that might have been.

When youth long past held promise fine,
As a pure girl offered love sublime,
When the world seemed decked in flowers gay,
No thorn to prick you in the way,
Just love & you, no bars between,
How grand to think what might have been.

When words you spoke in bitter vein,
Turned the joy of love to a cruel pain,
When two lives choosed apart to drift,
And spurned for aye God's greatest gift,
Yet as we sow so shall we glean,
But O the years that might have been.

When you feel the touch of Death's cold hand,
As your soul goes up to the Spirit land,
When a vision clear of a woman's face,
Seem to bridge those years now flown apace,
Could you recall those youthful days,
When life was bright with love's warm rays,
How pleasant now life's journey's end,
With her you spurned, as wife & friend,
Ah years! cruel years, in death is seen,
The perfect life which might have been.

At the end of the day

It is good to feel the hand of friend,
When day is drawing near its end,
And earth & sky together blend,
> At close of day.

It is good to know a kind act done,
When golden rays speaks setting sun,
And love with youth & health are one,
> At close of day.

It is good to ease an aching heart,
When sorrow fills life's greater part,
And faith grows dim & shadows start,
> At close of day.

It is good to rest when Death is near,
When the vision of Beyond is clear,
And Angels come to banish care,
> At close of day.

Major Wallace MC (with bar)
2/3rd Lon Fld Amb
Killed in action 27/3/18

Not a stouter heart not a braver man,
Left the shores of his native isle,
Not a better part in war's grim plan,
Was played in a nobler style.

No thought of self, of rank, or class,
Ambition, power, or gain,
But others first – himself the last,
His sorrow for their pain.

He smiled at danger, knew no fear,
His place was in the van,
He gave his best to heal & cheer,
His brother every man.

A gentleman he lived & died,
A 'right' man to the end,
Another World has gained a soul,
And we have lost a friend.

A tribute to the Infantry

When this big world-war is over,
When you live in peaceful days,
And you want to thank the 'Tommies',
I'll tell you whom to praise.
It's the bloke who had the roughest time
    with the Huns across the sea,
Who bore the brunt in every stunt,
    in the good old infantry.

Not a billet in some fancy town,
With a "posh" civilian bed,
But a groundsheet & a d____d hard floor,
In a draughty leaking shed.
When out on "rest" they had to work,
    (that's funny you'll agree),
They were served like that in every batt,
    in the good old infantry.

In the front line trenches every time,
(Not a deep dug-out behind),
He would have to stay & face the shells,
When "old Fritz" was most unkind,
In mud waist-deep, & sights like Hell,
      he stuck it splendidly,
With a lousey shirt, full of stinking dirt,
      in the good old infantry.

In a bombing raid in the dark & rain,
He would crawl across to Fritz,
For a bob a day, (or a little more),
And perhaps get blown to bits.
The Army's slave – Yes! Every day,
      He never felt quite free,
"Over the top" was his grim lot
      in the good old infantry.

You may call them soldiers whom you saw,
At the base with fancy clothes,
They were simply wrapped in cotton wool,
So they never got hard blows.
You would see them decked as a fashion-plate,
They had "posh" jobs, fared well,
And the war to them was a pleasant game,
For they never saw a shell.
So lift your glass, & raise a cheer,
For the chaps who bore the brunt,
Who had a d____d hard time all through,
And fought in every "stunt",
Let's honour those to whom it's due,
   it's up to you & me,
To shout "Well done!" to every one
   of the good old infantry.

Home

Where the wild-fowls call over marsh & fen,
And the breeze brings the taste of the sea,
Where the tracks are seen of the wild moor-hen,
And the rook's nest sway in the highest tree,
Where the pastures green brings rest to the eyes,
Where the seagulls skim o'er the foam,
And the corn turns to gold as the sunlight dies,
That's the place I would call my home.

Where the city's roar cannot jar on the ear,
And the noise of the crowd is unheard,
Where the lust of gold does not lay its snare
And the passions of men are not stirred,
Where the air is pure & love is true,
Where the lark sings its song of glee,
And springtime paints the earth anew,
That's the place where I long to be.

Where the rich soil calls to the plough & spade,
And the arms of the toilers grow strong,
Where the flowers bloom in the woodland glade,
And right takes the power from wrong,
Where the moon & the stars shine the clearer,
And the night-winds blow healthy & free,
Where man & his God are drawn nearer,
That's the place that is calling to me.

56th London Division

At call for right & justice, for freedom of the world,
'Gainst tyrant's proud ambition an Empire's might was hurled
For liberty of nations, for justice to the small,
From Britain's farthest outposts arose a clarion call,
And a mighty city answered with grim & firm intent
From shop, & desk, & office – The men of London went.

To Belgium's devastated soil, through Picardy's ruined land,
To blighted valley of the Somme (the mark of Hunnish hand),
'Midst hardship & discomfort, through pain & hellish sights,
In fierce & deadly battles, through grim uncertain nights,
Where German hosts were strongest on lust & ruin bent,
Where trusted troops were needed – The men of London went.

Remember mighty England, as ages pass away,
And future generations learn the history of today
When tyrants shall no longer reign to drench a world with blood,
But people of all nations shall form one brotherhood
When sacred memories of today shall future thoughts recall,
Of those who come from other lands to save the weak & small,
Remember then, with proud delight when Belgian homes were rent,
And the call came "do your duty" – The men of London went.

The Women of France

Long years of war & oppression,
Under the heel of the Huns,
Treated as vermin & cattle,
Hearing the voice of the guns,
Clothing & savings all taken,
Their protests arousing but mirth,
They bore all the hardship & suffering,
For the glorious land of their birth.

Parted from husband & brother,
Beaten, illtreated, & shamed,
Treated as beasts of burden,
Tortured, insulted, & maimed,
Undaunted, unflinching in spirit,
The "Tricolour" unfurled to the breeze,
Proving the Hun could not conquer,
The spirit of women like these.

All that was sacred & holy,
Their honour, their home, & their land,
Ruin & rape & destruction,
(The mark of the Hun devil's hand)
Defiant in face of tormentors,
Killed by the bayonet or lance,
Unconquered, Unbeaten, God bless them,
The women who did it for France.

To a Sandbag

"A friend in need is a friend indeed",
That's a proverb sound & true,
As home at last I watch the flames,
And think my love of you.

Though years have passed still memory clings,
To those hard distant days,
When you were with me staunch & true,
In all my varied ways.

'Gainst burning sun you were my shield,
When my tin hat drew heat,
And when the snow was on the ground,
You helped to warm my feet.

When hunger used to stalk my path,
To fill my heart with dread,
You proved a never-failing friend,
And held my daily bread.

When tired & worn through stress of work,
My body cried for rest,
Then sleep was sound & comforting,
As pillow you were best.

Though parted now I'll ne'er forget,
Those years across the sea,
The miles we tramped o'er trench & track,
And you were true to me.

Can you forget

There are incidents that happen in the lives of one & all,
They stand out clear as beacons & memories of recall,
We never shall forget the time, the place or fateful day,
If we live to reach an hundred & our head is bald or grey,
We may forget our martial life when discipline was strict,
But we shall all remember – that time we nearly "clicked"

Your memory may fail you of the roads you used to tramp,
Of the rations or the blankets in the "div" reception camp,
Or the little village café & the name of Mademoiselle,
Who would serve you with some stuff called beer & other drinks as well,
And those special trips to Paris, you've forgotten who were picked,
But it seems as clear as yesterday – that time you nearly "clicked"

It may have been at Cambrai or close to Armentières,
Where "old Fritz" would chuck the gas about & fill your eyes with tears,
No matter if you served in France, in Belgium, Palestine,
If you were coming out on rest or going in the line,
You may have seen a landmark – perhaps a tank, all derelict,
But all you can remember is – that time you nearly "clicked"

You've been along the Menin Road, the other side of Ypres,
Where the sight of "Hell Fire Corner" used to fill you with the creeps,
It may have been at Bullecourt or a shell-hole on the Somme,
When you thought you'd miss the roll-call & your time to die had come,
Or where the CT parapet had all been knocked away,
And your head would be a target for the Hun across the way,
You never can forget that time – Ah! how the seconds ticked,
And you'd got a proper "wind up" – that time you nearly "clicked"

I remember

I remember, I remember,
When going in the line,
The petrol can of water,
That nearly broke my spine.
It never seemed to fit my back,
Or was not water-tight,
But now I think of it each day,
And dream of it each night.

I remember, I remember,
The sandbag that I knew,
Which made a pillow for my head,
And held my rations too.
I always had a love for it,
And when we had to part,
I missed it not for many a day,
But now it grieves my heart.

I remember, I remember,
The buxom Mademoiselle,
And the little corner café,
In which she used to dwell,
I often had a talk with her,
But ah, those memories pale,
As with an English girl I sit,
And tell the same old tale.

I remember, I remember,
The leave train to the base,
And how it used to dash along,
A daring, reckless pace,
I often wondered at its speed,
Along the gleaming rail,
And now I pause & think of it,
Each time I see a snail.

56th London Division

I saw a batch of prisoners in a cage down Arras way,
(It was back in 1917 about the month of May),
I walked across & spoke to one, a chap with wiry hair,
And said "Hullo, young Hindenburg, how did you get in here?"
He hung his head & answered & his eyes were filled with tears,
"We tried to take a bit of trench from the Royal Fusiliers"

I left the cage of "Fritzes" & walked toward the line,
(I saw no "John Bull" Tommies who on steak & chips did dine),
But instead, a line of stretchers, each with a bandaged Hun,
So I stopped & asked the final man what foul deed had been done.
I said to him "Please tell me why you look such awful wrecks?"
"We tried to do a raid" he said, against the Middlesex.

In an O.P. near the front line trench I found myself at dawn,
The boys were going over at 6 o'clock that morn,
A village perched upon a ridge two thousand yards in front,
Was planned as their objective (it was going to be "some" stunt)
I watched the barrage open & I saw the boys set out,
And old Fritz sent up his fireworks & slung some stuff about.

At mid-day all was over & I knew the place was won,
They were coming in by hundreds, the mild & gentle Hun,
I smiled at one – a surly brute – a Prussian NCO,
He looked a pretty picture with mud from head to toe.
"You couldn't stop our boys?" I asked, his face went very red,
He looked at me in anger & this is what he said.
"We tried to hold the village, but I ask, what could we do?
With your L.R.B.'s upon us & your Queens Westminsters too,
We have met them many times before, the Kensingtons as well,
And those London Scottish devils who always give us Hell,
The "black list" that our Kaiser has of troops we have to fear,
Has grown to be a long one & the 56th is there"
He broke out into cursing, I left the fellow then,
And as I walked away he said "Gott straffe your London men"

The other works of Alick Lewis Ellis

(found among the belongings of his late brother
Clarence Allen Ellis and his late nephew Robert Ellis)

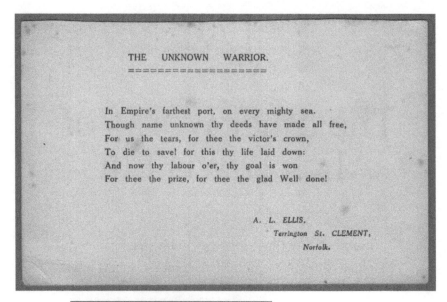

THE UNKNOWN WARRIOR.

In Empire's farthest port, on every mighty sea.
Though name unknown thy deeds have made all free,
For us the tears, for thee the victor's crown,
To die to save! for this thy life laid down:
And now thy labour o'er, thy goal is won
For thee the prize, for thee the glad Well done!

A. L. ELLIS,
Terrington St. CLEMENT,
Norfolk.

The poem 'Unknown Warrior', printed on the back of a 'Winox, Wine food' postcard

THE UNKNOWN WARRIOR

In Empire's farthest port, on every mighty sea.
Though name unknown thy deeds have made all free,
For us the tears, for thee the victor's crown,
To die to save! for this thy life laid down:
And now thy labour o'er, thy goal is won
For thee the prize, for thee the glad Well done!

> A.L. Ellis
> Terrington St. CLEMENT,
> Norfolk

VICTORY

Ring out the bells to herald in the light.
Lift Victory's banner o'er the earth again,
That peoples of the World may know that right
Still stands triumphant after falsehood's reign.

Hoist Freedom's flag on heights that all may see
That Truth and Justice over all the Earth hold sway,
That races, creeds, and innocents are free,
That darkest night has born a glorious day.

Light up the beacons on the mountain's crest,
That tortured slaves may know the storm has passed,
That all mankind shall be by Heaven blessed
With Liberty and Freedom that shall last.

Roll muffled drums for men of stirling worth
Who rest in peace in many an alien land.
They gave their all to make a better Earth,
Crusaders in the fight 'gainst tyrant's hand.

Let future years remember men of fame
Who freely gave, that we might live in Peace,
And children yet to be shall bless their name,
And hatred by mankind for ever cease.

Alick L Ellis

The original poem 'Victory' signed by Alick Ellis. The signature matches that of his RAMC registration paper

VICTORY

Ring out the bells to herald in the light.
Lift victory's banner o'er the earth again,
That peoples of the World may know that right
Still stands triumphant after falsehood's reign.

Hoist Freedom's flag on heights that all may see
That Truth and Justice over all the Earth hold sway,
That races, creeds, and innocents are free,
That darkest night has born a glorious day.

Light up the beacons on the mountain's crest,
That tortured slaves may know the storm has passed,
That all mankind shall be by Heaven blessed
With Liberty and Freedom that shall last.

Roll muffled drums for men of stirling worth
Who rest in peace in many an alien land.
They gave their all to make a better Earth,
Crusaders in the fight 'gainst tyrant's hand.

Let future years remember men of fame
Who freely gave, that we might live in Peace,
And children yet to be shall bless their name,
And hatred by mankind for ever cease.

Alick L Ellis

REAL GREATNESS
Composed by Alick L Ellis

You may not hold the magic key,
    That opens society's gate
Or climb the ladder men call success
    Or ride in the ship of state
You may pass un-noticed amid'st the crowd
    Unknown to the mass on earth
And those that hold to the power of gold
    may deem you of little worth.

Let the world go round in its same old way
    You do not need its praise
If you have a smile and a word of cheer
    For the fallen on life's highway
If those that are crushed by the mills of greed
    You help to start anew
To all in need prove a friend indeed
    There's nothing wrong with you

If you pause a while as you hear the sound
    Of children at their play
If they run to you and take your hand
    As you pass along their way
Or show their playthings without fear
    As children love to do
You'll understand as they take your hand
    There's nothing wrong with you

If the weak and worn through weight of years
    Should feel their yoke too strong
And you lend your aid in a modest way
    To help them pass along
If you brighten days that mark their end
    As they draw near the fold
If you stand for right in the world's great fight
    You are worth a price untold.

(found among the belongings of Mr Robert Ellis – nephew to Alick)

Acknowledgements

At a moment such as this, it is only right to first acknowledge Alick himself. For someone growing up in the quiet environment of a small Norfolk village we can only guess at the experiences and personal images of war that led to him producing such compelling poetry. Often dark, but sometimes lined with humour, with each different poem we are given a small insight into an often destructive and harrowing environment. It would be impossible not to acknowledge the physical and emotional trauma of so many and to wonder, even for those who returned, just how much of every soldier was left behind.

100 years on from its writing and our heartfelt thanks go out to the anonymous person who found and so kindly handed in Alick's book to the Herts at War Project. It would have been so simple to keep it, out of curiosity, a momento of a house renovation. But thankfully no, your kindness has enabled us to publish these works, so that they can be seen by all and in turn support fitting charitable causes.

To Dan Hill at the Herts at War Project who tracked down Bob Ellis, Alick's closest living relative so that the original book could be returned to the family, we say a huge thank you. During the few times we have spoken or met, your enthusiasm has been enourmous and the insights you gave us into the RAMC and the Western Front in general were invaluable.

So little has been recorded about Alick's life. He spoke little if anything about his experiences in France, and the only personal recollections of him came from our father Bob Ellis who in the last months of life recounted the few stories we have.

We would like to thank the staff of the Museum of Military Medicine in Aldershot for their encouragement to publish these poems, and to our family and friends whose continued support has been instrumental throughout the whole process.

And finally, we would like to say many thanks to our publishers SPP, and in particular Heather Morris who has guided us to produce the finished article you see today. We hope that the contribution from all these people has helped the reader to experience a full spectrum of emotions generated by "Field Dressings, by Stretcher Bearer".